Trigger

an a

blood
moon
POETRY

Trigger Warning

Cover art by Kerry Squires
ISBN: 978-1-7399155-3-7
Imprint: blood moon POETRY

for the women who feel unsafe, unheard and unvalued
for all women, today and always

Trigger Warning

Note from the Guest Editor

We all have a story. According to WHO across their lifetime, 1 in 3 women, around 736 million, are subjected to physical or sexual violence by an intimate partner or sexual violence from a non-partner. That's what the statistics say, but my life experience would say every woman has, and most of the women in my life have multiple stories. In 2021 male violence felt more present than ever - the UK was rocked by harrowing story after harrowing story. We all know the cases of Sabina Nessa, Bibaa Henry, Nicole Smallman and Sarah Everard. But there are hundreds we don't know, of women killed by their partners, of trans women who aren't included in many of the statistics, of women of colour who often don't get the press white women do. A report by Femicide Census found that one woman is killed every three days in the UK.

In the last decade more than nine out of 10 killers in the UK were men. About 57% of female victims were killed by someone they knew, most commonly a partner or ex-partner. While there were 52,210 rapes recorded by police in England and Wales in 2020, only 843 resulted in a charge or a summons – a rate of 1.6%. I'm listing these statistics as a precursor - because every time I've spoken out against male violence and sexual assault, I'm told it's rare. That I'm overreacting. That it only happens to women who aren't careful. The onus is always placed on women. But it is so very real, and so very terrifying - women are conditioned to live their lives trying to avoid being killed, assaulted and raped by men, and constantly finding that it is impossible - because it is done to us, and allowed to continue, largely unpunished, because of the patriarchal society we live in. Sometimes it's easy to feel powerless - when the government isn't helping enough, when most men are silent, when we have massive cultural conversations that lead nowhere. But, sharing our stories, supporting each other and campaigning for change will make a difference, bit by bit.

The proceeds for this collection are being donated to the 'Rape Crisis England & Wales' charity, which is a feminist organisation that supports the work of Rape Crisis Centres across England and Wales, who also work to raise awareness and understanding of sexual violence and abuse in all its forms.

Trigger Warning

Trigger Warning is a collection of poems by survivors, documenting their stories - our stories - some have written of the microaggressions that women face daily that normalise sexual violence, or the feelings of not being believed, others have shared the details of their rape, of their triggers following an assault. Every poem is unique, themes echoing but details differing. The process of collating this anthology has felt intentional at every step. blood moon POETRY had an open submission, where over one hundred wonderful poems were submitted. The other editors and I selected which could make this anthology - a hard but rewarding task - where we sifted blind. For me, this has been such an important part of this journey; I believe that poetry should be accessible, and in my own small way I am trying to help rid the poetry world of its elitism and superiority. So, an open and blind submission felt fair, it made this collection about the stories and words not about who got what degree or accolade.

As the title suggests, this collection comes with a massive trigger warning and having edited each of these poems, I know how important it is to take your time reading these. But I hope that you find them as helpful as I have - to see words in print about stories we are told not to speak of is so very powerful. And validating. It is not our shame to hold, to be beaten with.

With love,

Chloe
find me @chloegracelaws and @fgrlsclub

Trigger Warning

Trigger Warning

Note from the Editor

I began writing this note with the phrase 'after the death of Sabina Nessa' and then, I stopped. Re-read that line and realised I had joined countless others in excusing or explaining away her murder with that one inaccurate phrase. So, it is in fact the truth to say here, that this anthology wouldn't exist had it not been for the murder of Sabina Nessa. This book is in your hands and you are reading these poems, because violence against women is an epidemic. Every day and all over the world, this is not just a problem unique to the United Kingdom: no corner of contemporary society is undarkened.

Yet it wasn't mainstream reporting that brought Sabina to my attention, but a post being shared on Instagram by journalist Katrina Mirpuri who I happened to follow. Searching for her name on news sites brought up stories that were just a few lines long and buried at the bottom of most pages. Still today it remains the work of women who refuse to be silenced and resist the pull of what is considered traditional or 'appropriate', to keep saying the names of those who are disappearing. No. Those who are being disappeared.

When we decided to open a short submission window after the murder of Sabina, we were also putting together another book and so could only manage a three-day process. In that time, we expected a small number of poems to come in, especially given that we were asking for women to write about their experiences with sexual assault and violence. Though we knew the statistics (20% of women have experienced some type of sexual assault since the age of 16*), we weren't sure that the women in our community would want to write about or share their work on this topic. Yet by the time submissions closed, we had received over 100 poems with more emails and DMs coming in after the deadline (and still today) asking if it was too late to send something.

Along with their poems, many women sent us their stories. By way of contextualising their work, explaining why it would be so brutal and confronting to read their words or – in many cases – simply to say thank you for giving them a place to put their work. A number of poets included here have never shared their experience with anyone and so, this is more than a poetry anthology.

Trigger Warning is not just a book of poems, it has become the collective voice that tells the world just what it is to be a woman surviving today.

It goes without saying that every woman on the editorial board of blood moon POETRY is exceptionally proud to have steered this book from conception to publication. As Editor-in-chief, I am humbled to be co-introducing this collection along with Chloe Grace Laws. Our hope is that Trigger Warning can stand as a marker in time and a tool with which we begin to turn the tide of change for all women. With our fundraising partner Rape Crisis England & Wales, our aim is to ensure all proceeds of this book go towards supporting women who are victims and survivors of sexual assault and violence.

Not every rape or sexual assault ends in murder. But every time a woman is made to feel unsafe it is as though we are being told our life means nothing.

Our mission at blood moon POETRY has always been to raise the volume on women's words above the noise that seeks to drown us out. This book is the loudest collection we have published so far. It is our way of advocating for the women whose words are written here and for all women who have been made to feel as though they are disposable. Trigger Warning is brought to you with courage, truth and hope. Take care as you read it. And then, join us in demanding more for women.

Lunar love,
Holly Ruskin
Editor-in-chief & co-founder
blood moon POETRY

*www.rapecrisis.org.uk/get-informed/about-sexual-violence

Trigger Warning

Trigger Warning

Contents

Trigger Warning

Foreword

In this anthology, the voices of women come alive as they share their darkest moments with you. The weight they've carried with them is transferred through the text and you may even find that each page feels heavier with each turn.

As the name suggests, Trigger Warning is not a light read, however, it is essential reading. You've heard stories like this before in the news and on social media, but when you hear them one after the other it's as if you're being invited to read diary entries. Words are carefully selected, spelling out what you might have been too afraid to think of.

It is apparent that change is overdue. The underlying theme of violence and injustice is one that evokes anger. But, if there's something you can take away from this, it's that trauma creates a strong bond. I believe this bond is the key to ending violence against women. Forget blood brothers. We are sisters, bound together, feeling every blow like a punch in the gut.

I felt this bond for the first time after the death of Sabina Nessa. I felt rage when her name was not plastered on pages and screens. I took my anger online. I channeled it through words (the only way I know) guiding people to a post that was titled "read me". Her name needed to be heard. It didn't take long for women to flood my inbox. They shared the information fast, and absorbed the gory details. Women organised local vigils. Women came out of the woodwork, lit their torches and walked with each other, no questions asked. We stood together and held candles in the square and walked each other home. Many asked "where is the support from men?". There are no brownie points for showing up, but so many did. Believe me when I say that there was quite the army!

We were there for her, and the one before, and the one before and for each other. Despite the never ending violence, we still remain. Although Trigger Warning's nature is sinister, there's a warmth to the text that might comfort you. It feels as if you're alone with each woman writing the poem, sitting opposite them sipping a cup of tea, or a glass of wine as they tell you what happened.

A clean exchange. Stories to hold close and use as fuel for future progress.

Katrina Mirpuri

Trigger Warning

If I Die By Male Violence

Erin Darcy

If I die by Male Violence
I don't want you to be silent
I want a riot

I don't want candles gathered around
I want you to burn everything down.

A bonfire and flaming torches to the sky
I don't want it be asked "How Did She Die"
I want it screamed WHY

Why men think they are entitled to our smile. To our chat. Why men think they are entitled to our bodies. To our time. Why men think they are entitled to our spaces, to our celebrations. Why men think they are entitled to our achievements, our independence, ingenuity, and strength. Why men think they are entitled to make laws. Why men think they are entitled to set the tone. Why men think they are entitled to tell a woman to calm down. Why men think they are fucking entitled. Why men? Why.

Why is it our mess to clean up
Why is it ours to educate?
Why

I don't need my achievements read aloud
As if that is all I'm worth
I want the man found,
and his name and blood stained across this earth.

These are the sons of patriarchy
Fragile masculinity.
May they never live a moments peace.

So please don't hold a moments silence
If I die by male violence.
I want a riot.

Trigger Warning

Boys In Blue Blazers

Chloe Laws

Boys in blue blazers called me by my last name
Trading cigarettes and blowjobs for their approval
        taken back once they'd taken me
It was always about power. before I knew that power
        wasn't always married to super.
When I thought it was something only old men in high castles had
Not schoolboys sat on church pews

Trigger Warning

Things I Saw When I Wanted To Say No

Yvonne Gavan

polyester stripe of my checkout dress/ bike against the bedroom wall/ cider and black/ hand on the back of a plastic chair/ your eye a slice of your fringe in the glass/ Camden candle in confetti red/ cloudy night sky/ sun lounger springs/ smoke on lips/ yellow wall/ a safety poster/ pavement cracks and my black school shoes/ a mouth full of milk teeth gaps/ and a mouth that said "be good" and "do as you're told"/ a ginger cat/ a corduroy knee/ a line in a book about girls who fail that sticks and sticks

Trigger Warning

Savage Beauty

Tetyana Denford

are those mountains
or clouds, I think
both have sharp peaks
both white and pure, both make me sigh
at how beautiful the world can be
when you close your hand over my mouth
and tell me
to be quiet
you see, I don't remember much of things
like your belt buckle knocking against my teeth
or swallowing my voice
or the muffled loudness
of the lock on your door
I remember asking if the world
would ever hold more
for me.
And that's when the sky whispered
look over here
and find beauty.

Trigger Warning

I didn't know

Holly Ruskin

I think the saying goes
that a tree falls though
without ears to hear the
crash it may as well
have stayed upright
root in earth

because if it can't be heard
then it didn't happen and
I *didn't* make a sound then*

      (couldn't know I'd fallen)

yes it's only now I *think*
it happened
(that tiny crack *was* my splitting in two)

and though no one heard it
not even me
I realise...

no.

I know.

I was cut
      down

                  except the moans I had to make

Trigger Warning

Lemons

Jaimee Boake

with a whiff of lemon-scented dish soap
I'm back on cobbled streets in Capri

rough hand heavy on arm/that smile that didn't reach hard eyes/and
I shivered as he squeezed/ my throat itched to be louder/a second
stretched to years/sudden stinging slice of hidden knife

/ makes blood mix with soapy water down the kitchen sink drain

maybe when I learn to say
let me go
in fifty languages
the fear will be washed from me too

Trigger Warning

Decisions

Eleanor Fatharly

Never had a usual at the local.
People pleaser through nature
Shapeshifter through necessity.

In a world full of choice
I am hungry.

I still know
that I chose no.

Trigger Warning

Love Language

Tahlia McKinnon

I am sitting on his front step, the first time that I tell him. The brickwork rough beneath my bare knees. He says that I look ugly when I cry. Takes my hand in his and bites the palm until it bleeds. Smears it on my cheeks like warpaint. [I would live inside of your mouth if I could. I know.] He walks me home. I count the cracks in the concrete. Calm before the storm. Words ricocheting off the curb. [Hear that? Even the earth wants to swallow you. I know.] That night, I dream of snow. I am buried deep beneath the sheet. A bloodied mess, my head between my legs. It is agony. It is beautiful. A week later, I welcome him to my bed. He says that I am cold inside, just like the dead. It is agony. It is beautiful. He finishes. Smears it on my chin like a baptism. [And you should be grateful. I know.] I walk him home. He asks me if it hurts, but I'm not sure where. We stop beneath a streetlamp, his fingers through my hair. [You have no idea; what people do to each other. But I could show you. I know.] And he does. Turns out some stains show up best in the dark. I live there now.

Trigger Warning

Modern Womanhood in 5 Senses

Grace Dellis

Sight

I am 12 years old when I am ushered
into modern womanhood / the first
unsolicited dick pic arriving just after
my first period / Welcome to the 21st century.

Touch

I have given my phone number
to a man out of sheer politeness / and he
begins to stalk me; he feels the sting
of rejection / and I feel the ice
from his glass as it hits my face.

Taste

I drink tequila / bold and ringing
on my tongue / and the night is bitter
static around me / every other sensation
lost to a person I will never know; I taste
tequila for days afterward / as if the bile
is trying to remember what happened to me.

Sound

I hear clear as a clanging bell and
just as sturdy / my boyfriend's angry fists
pounding on my locked and rattling door
after I jump from his still-moving car;
I hear his voice / clear as a clanging bell /
though not as bright or shiny / as he recounts
every wrong thing I have done.

→

Smell

I am in a cloud of smoke and body odour
as the drunk asks to hold my hand / late
at night on an empty train / as I walk
the platform to the sound of "whore"
screamed from schoolboy mouths / as I
sit on an airplane next to a man
twice my age who tries to stick his finger
in my ear while I sleep.

Trigger Warning

Distorted Sunrise

CC Rose

Distorted by the sunrise,
These high-rise shadows cast a doubt
They invite my demise.

Within the towering blocks that touch the blue
Something deeper lags behind
My understanding of life.

The bruises braised across my cheek, my thighs
This swollen rib reflects last night
A croaky voice - shaken by fright - stays distorted.

The mirrors I project are only there to let beauty shine.
The image of me is not who I am,
Not the same one who stands.
Within this reality hides the thought;
'But he loves me, he couldn't, he wouldn't do that to me'.

In Which My Grapefruit Looks Too Much Like Me

Solo

I stab my spoon into the wedge
dusted with a thick layer of sugar
the granules wet—a sudden, thin burst
an almost-pink leaking across the mound.
I watch everything bleed,
clump together. I force it out,
spoon cutting as clean as a scalpel
a gentle curve to the outside,
sharp slice to the inside,
thrust it underneath.
Ah, that semicircle of sweet flesh
watch me pop it in my mouth.

I'm just a little hungry,
searching for what they all were—
just a little bit of juice to show
I'm not doing this entirely wrong.

It's enough to justify
one layer devoured,
then a second,
then a third
then I'm moving too quick,
a spurt catches me in the eye
like a small act of vengeance
but I keep going.

→

Trigger Warning

The hallowed half stares up at me,
pip speckled chin, pale forearms dribbling
in a weak effort to replenish
its layers of thick, translucent skin
exposed
collapsing on each other
like a bitter torn vulva.

There is no fruit, yet
I have eaten nothing.

Trigger Warning

Trigger Warning

Well Deserved

Stephanie Moore

When
the man
on the tube
was intruding my personal space
I felt unable to say a word
like
when my friend's husband
put his hand up my skirt
for a bit of harmless flirting
and
isn't it absurd
that our worth
is tied up in a body
that doesn't seem to be
only our property?
openly owned
by the men who invent
reasons
to have
'meetings'
so they can teach us
what it is
to feel uneasy
breeching professional boundaries
until you're found
drugged back at their house
and somehow
you
take the blame
always the same slut-shaming
your age made you an adult
so why can't you learn your lesson?

→

be
less suggestive
re-direct their advances
don't be so dramatic
just stop dressing for attackers
watch your back more
don't
walk through the park
when it's quiet
or dark
mark out a route
and share it to prove
you knew you'd done
everything you could
to be a good girl

because look
they'll call you clueless
and foolish
for wearing the 'wrong shoes'
or ignoring what happened in the news
Surely
you realised
it could have easily been you!
See
All of us are asking for it
When one man behind a tree
Won't allow us our freedom
Because he can't
Keep his fists or his
Stupid little prick or his frikkin
ego neatly in check
they couldn't care less
about our protection
collectively saying
oh! it's just another day
when a young lady
walked the wrong way
stupidly

→

refused to change her behaviour
maybe if she had
he wouldn't have raped her
so the blame's on her
silly girl
and
for what it's worth
I mean
did you see the length of her skirt??!
seriously…
she probably fucking deserved it.

Just My Age

Stephanie Moore

At a party.
Drink drunk.
Drugs offered.
you should take them.
Got to fit in
Don't know what?
Didn't check.
My fault.
I was young.
Just my age.
Wearing a dress.
Not that short.
But. Too short?
My choice.
New to the scene
Told- 'you
Need to be seen'.
By adults
shaping my career.
Came to my home.
I opened the door.
Music on.
a come on?
I was young
they were old
like an uncle
and my dad.
sad, that I trusted
My fault?
I trusted them. him.
with my dream
the father figure
groping me
I said no, i think
but maybe not
loud enough

$\rightarrow$

Strong enough
right enough
sure enough
he left. not soon enough
and the uncle one
said, I'm sorry about him
But
But /

memory turns off
clothes were off
on the bed
is he on top?
And then
He is rushing off
before the sun is up
and he is saying sorry
I'll go I'm sorry
and not looking me in the eyes
and I'm not sure if I'm even alive
if this is even me
in this mad
panicked moment
It is hot and foggy
and I wander aimlessly from
room to room
And when I wake up it's
Afternoon
and I look at my phone
and I'm crying

Crying and crying
Face wetter than ever
Pacing, my heart is racing
Because I can't remember
what happened.
what even
what time is it
What day is it
I'm not ok

→

what is it, what is this?
He was meant
to write me a part
in a play
Not invade
Not stay

not

take everything away.

Trigger Warning

They Too Become Hands

Seneca Basoalto

What you don't know is that I have watched myself fall through the trees,
fleeing from hands that have spun webs around my throat & named it nocturne.

I think about hands. I dream about hands / My teeth become fists &
failures that gnaw through unspoken words / I sleep, only to wake up
to hands / I breathe hands / I become obsessed with hands beyond the
memory of a busted knuckle shoved into my mouth.

My mouth, freckled too, also hands, they hear his death threats through
the static & suddenly recall they taste like Marlboro & Beaujolais.
His death threats reshape from words he uses in each of his songs, so
they too become hands that maneuver slow motion through the .07
seconds it takes me to notice his posture
the curl of crooked fingers make a crown.

He moves through me; I am a pasture / this is the same thing as prey.
What am I? If he is me that means I am mine / if he is me, I am only
allowed to speak to myself. If he is me, as he claims to be, then I live in
fear of my own hands. Like father, like daughter. Like rivers, like blood.
Like lovers, like hunters. If I do not break my fingers to answer the
phone, then I might as well slip into the tub & not wake up.

What you don't know is that I do not have to be near him
to know that if I breathe,
he will hear it
If I breathe the wrong way,
I will never breathe again.

Trigger Warning

Treasures

Catherine Bartram

Sometimes I feel tarred
Stuck in a fug
Dredging depths
Dare you to comprehend
what hasn't already been dug
Feathers stuck to me
like a glue
Pluck away
at that day
The recurring one
where you tested my sanity
Pushing shoving
Lying stealing
Smashing kicking
Shouting spitting
Snarling rarling
Stalking

This monster
Who tried to destroy
my life daily
My generational steel
propelled me
knowing hoping praying
The best is yet to come
And growth is good
Not bad
To hurt and to heal is
Healing

The Naked Truth

Melanie Hess

Deliberately, patiently circling
an updraft carries my scent your way
you spot me
and know what you will do

Salivating
you take a seat upon my table
feasting long and luxuriously
sticky fingers mould my flesh,
teeth scrape my bones
until nothing remains but scraps
and dirty plates.

You pluck the wishbone from between my legs
a trophy
engraved with my innocence

you know what you have done.

Trigger Warning

GIVE IT A NAME

Kait Quinn

It took me years to give it a name. To call it what it was. To label it "violent," even though there were never any bruises or fractures, not a single drop of blood to show for it. How many more years will it take to name it out loud?

A decade later, and I still can't talk about it. Can't even write about it because he'll read it, then tell me that it was my fault or that I remembered it wrong, but it wasn't and I didn't. I swear I didn't. In the morning he said, "It felt like I was raping you." Sometimes, I still get it: how you can feel but not know. Blame it on my love. Blame it on the alcohol. Blame it on all the ways that I am too weak to bother fighting anyone off.

And I still can't talk about that one night at the Holiday Inn across the lake from downtown Austin because I still don't believe it was enough to call it what it was. I still believe it was my fault. I deserved it. I swear I did. If you knew the lies and all the vodka and bad choices, you'd believe it too. I don't know what was dream, what was wake. Couldn't find the light switch in the windowless bathroom. Couldn't find the nerve to crawl from his groping hands off the bed, out the door, across 35 in the direction of home. But it scarred me enough to inch away from love's touch to this day. To toss my favorite dress in the garbage first thing the next morning.

I wish I could spill it all. Wish I could expose that corner of my heart and let the poison finally leak from bloodstream. Wish I could be as brave as all the fire-breathing goddesses in this arms-open, we-got-your-back, no-judgment-here poetry circle. It's not that I don't trust you. It's that I don't trust myself. It's that I still don't believe me. It's that I still think I put too much weight onto nothing. It's that other women have known worse and I should shut my needy mouth.

I know one day I'll see that it was real and it matters and there's no such thing as comparison when it comes to something like this. One day I'll be ready to pour every secret out with the dirty bathwater. But for now, it's just safer to sweep it away like a bad dream. Because it still feels insignificant enough to have only been that—just a bad dream that won't rest.

Trigger Warning

No Saint

Emma Taylor

I do not forgive you
Even if that makes me ugly
I am no beatific saint
Blinking down at you
through bloody tears
I am the animal you wounded
Mine's a memory
Of an ancient sea thing
And these scars
Would gape and seethe
Rather than please.
Let sleeping dogs lie, you said.
And lie they will!
I snarled.
Lie and lie forever!

Trigger Warning

Kate McAlister

sunlight on a
September afternoon
potentially disturbing
content on the way back home
please do not push
the button
before these thoughts come to a halt
green light and a burst of grey smog
wafting
I choke
this perfume -
you know
the one in the blue bottle
shaped like a man
not a headless monster
the stench of a
past rotting beneath
my ribs
each step still rattling

and yet I am once again
thrown flat on my back
drowning under that heavy body crushing me
twice my age
twice my size
the pavement melts into my mind
what a surprise to find
my twisted spine still upright
I don't freeze as I used to
but it still sets the world on fire

the weak flesh falling off my bones
these hands
once again
on my throat
and wrists

61

shaking
not like leaves in a storm
I bend over my mind
and the earth quakes
opens
with the rolling thunder
of my sisters whispering

You are not alone
You fight for me, too.

Trigger Warning

Trigger Warning

The Man Who Shouts

Rosie Szumowski

The man who shouts "nice legs darlin'!" at me whilst I'm walking to pick
up a pint of milk –
he doesn't care about me.

The one who shouts "how does that taste darlin'? You want something
else to chew on?" as I rush between two appointments at work and eat
my lunch as I go –
he doesn't care about me.

He'll purposefully get in my way to tell me he thinks I'm beautiful –
but he doesn't care about me.

SORRY / BITCHES

Ivana Kalaš

I fight men
I fight men in bars
I fight men in my head
I fight men in the streets
in uniforms
piss-soaked alleyways
and in bedrooms

I fight men   in relationships
mine or theirs

I'm called insane
I am insane

sorry your boyfriend is scared of me now
sorry I had to punch his friend
sorry he didn't have better friends
sorry he wasn't a better boyfriend
sorry I had to punch his friend
sorry I had to punch
sorry I had to pass on that behavior
that punched me
that made me punch

sorry I'm saying sorry
sorry that I'm not sorry
sorry that I actually am sorry
sorry that I learned to hate myself
sorry that I don't use my words

sorry that my voice is too shrill
sorry that it carries
sorry that it didn't carry when it mattered
sorry that I didn't scream
        that I pleaded
        I begged for the next punch not to kill me

→

Trigger Warning

I'm not sorry I want to prove to myself that
I took every punch and
I stored that energy in my neck in my shoulders in my readied muscles
just waiting for the next man
 (you)
to call me a
crazy bitch

Trigger Warning

Trigger Warning

Survivorhood

R S Kendle

It was done to me.

Yet it is I who must shoulder
This burden through life.
The one who must explain.

Explain myself.
Explain what happened.
Explain you.

I can barely find all the words.

Barely contain that little part of you /
That I must always carry.

You cling deep in the folds of my brain
Nesting somewhere between
The pre-frontal cortex and the temporal lobe.

I have forgotten so much of my childhood:
The smell of my Grannie's tattie soup,
The feel of a hand-knitted jumper on my skin.

But not you.

Never you.

Arrogant fingers,
Vinegary red-wine breath,
The sensation of my stomach solidifying.

I've shared this story so many times.

And it never gets easier.

Trigger Warning

Just Another [X] Poem

Kristina Rose Garcia

If I have to ask permission,
when he
never did -

There's a problem.

When people praise your stories of strength
in sickness or in chemo,
It's allowed -

Even he knows.

That is why it keeps
on
happening;

This is why
little girls cry in secret;
because this horror
you don't want to hear or see -

We have to keep it.

I have to tiptoe through life carrying the shame
and you continue to enable the same.

Five-year-old me could have heard it,
had a word for it -

But there aren't many words for that,
are there?

Not when people like you
shush me
when I tell about the violation under there,
in my underwear,

→

that he would rip off a helpless child.

Yet I need your permission to speak his decisions.

I had no choice -

Not then;

Not now.

Trigger Warning

Trigger Warning

Sixth Grade

Amy Soricelli

Did you think I wouldn't remember you when
the heat becomes a sidewalk fire that curls its tongue at me?
When the bitter cold is a knife at my throat?
Did you think you'd ever be gone from my head?
You're my lazy pulse.
I still keep my back to the wall because of you.
No one is ever behind me.
Did you know that?

I bet you didn't know you can be so many places at the same time.
I wonder if you cared that your scent stayed on my neck.
I wonder if you thought of that as you pulled your socks on from some
lost room of your dreary Bronx apartment.
You got ready for school just like me.
Did you live in this world?
You made the air grow sideways.
The snow landed warm.

You would lift up my skirt like your fingers had the right.
I was yours to touch.
A tall, skinny 11-year-old on her way to science.
I missed a year of frogs and smoke clouds, foggy
beakers and volcanos made of sand.

Did you think that years later, when I was standing in
line, I would turn, and turn, and turn?
I wonder if you had a mother, and if she gave you breakfast before
you headed out to the staircase.
Did you tell her about me?
What words did you use to tell her
how you would change my life forever.

Tell them to me now.
I could use them.

Trigger Warning

You

Claire Thom

You
stole handfuls of my breath
when your pitiful palms grappled
with my muted screams

took a pocketful of my innocence
when your pathetic fingers fumbled
with my youthful hips

snatched a bag full of my confidence
when your poor hands struggled
with my personal possessions

robbed an eyeful of my optimism
when your paltry nails scratched
at the surface of my naivety -

that obscure night
on that solitary street.

I
found strength
in the shadows

held courage
in clenched fists

discovered determination
stuck to my soles

felt my power
roar

→

Trigger Warning

You
scurried off
limp tail between your legs -

that obscure night
on that solitary street

Trigger Warning

Non-Anniversary

Sophia Murray

Superglued pieces of porcelain
Once fractured limbs
Hidden lines of memories
Best forgotten

I cradle myself
On this non-anniversary
Ink scars make it real
again and again

It only lives in my head
In the filing cabinet
In the back of my neck
Weighed down with love

For myself
I paste over the cracks
Easily broken
again I heal

Trigger Warning

Engulf

Alley Shubert

Georgia held me in her palm
then bit deep like the peaches we ate
that night in a field of sunsets.

This is how something so beautiful
could hurt so bad.

Ten years later and it still comes back
in snippets. How I stepped out of my skin
to let it dry on the radiator.

Seeds were sowed and
the woman was planted.
Roots tugged like a skirt.

19-year-old me ---
Please forgive me for insisting it
was all your fault.
For allowing you to carry shame &
to initiate blame.

I would like to say:
Let bygones be bygones.
Let the chips fall where they may.

That this poem is still about you.

That this poem can move mountains
& engulf the flames of one million
forest fires.

Too Bad

Abigail Elizabeth Ottley

The first thing I remember is you
grilling bacon, those mornings
when I wagged off school.

After two or three times I stopped
wanting to do it but couldn't
find the words to say
No.

I was smart for my age, though.
I did what you wanted, understood
more than you thought I did.

I knew your anger weighed
your heart like a whetstone
anticipated sparks.

Before you took your hunting knife
to hack off my hair I had slipped
too far from the surface.

I had so much lost my grip
there was no easy way I could haul
myself up to the light.

But I loved your kitchen with its
eye-level grill and that much bacon
was unheard of in our house.

With what tenderness you turned
each pink spitting rasher, how meticulous
your clearing up after.

It was a while before I realised
you feared your mother who worked
every day until four.

Making Reservations

Sarah Brooks

My body remains unceded
to men who would take
what is not theirs,
putting themselves
between the legs
of adolescent girls.
Groping hands, greedy

eyes that violate, inflict or
imply violence. Repeatedly
we are told our worth lies
in being desired-
Virginity traded for trinkets,
under blankets of dis-ease,
recovering untold shame.

My body had not yet seen
twenty years of age
when my first child
emerged from my womb
((contracting))
without my consent,
placing me in a position

of both strength
and dependence, constantly
calculating strategies
to extricate myself
from occupation by
addicts, who would use
manipulation against me.

I refused to raise my baby
in the pollution of the mainstream.
Yearning for community,
following trails of breadcrumbs,

→

I found my way
far into the woods to escape
what they call civilization.

I fled from that place where
it is deemed civilized
 To leave humans on the street
 To treat people as property
 To imply children are a choice
when no one cares
what you would choose.

A man can colonize
your uterus
and walk away- unscathed,
oblivious to the lives
left in harm's way
but I reserve the right
to decide my own fate.

My Mother Cries

Cat Balaq

My mother cries, tells me
she will take the child.
I am too young to be good
a pomegranate swallowed
swollen and wild- or I must go
- disowned. I cannot leave him.
We live alone. The man from
the farm hears me howl
every night, he taps my window,
pushes his lips through the crack
sucks tenderly a kiss,
nothing taken but haste.
I am told he has had
half his brain removed
but not the half that
would make him a man.
Motor accident, he claims,
C shape scar cut curved
across his cranium. I don't
admit what his mouth says
but know his body's dearth.
I curl up in the cancer of his
advance, just one of many
to ply their secondhand chance.
Men have taken their boldness out
at me on over hanging balconies,
behind secluded rock bays
posted cut outs from magazines,
sticky, I am not old enough to buy.
I have never been sent flowers.
A man has taken his firmness
out of me, leaving himself behind
squalling in my arms, in a green fold,
and I have never loved anything as much
not even half as much, every sickly
touch endured to bear this plum reward.

Fifteen

Victoria Davies

There is a small part of me
That is still fifteen years old
I'm not sure that part will ever grow up.
She is stuck worrying about how she looks
How she appears to others
And whether it's OK that her boyfriend
Steals her money and calls her names.
She isn't sure that it's meant to happen
But wonders if perhaps she deserves it.
If she was thinner
Prettier
More subservient
More like the other girls
The ones in the magazine he likes
With the plastic smiles and huge breasts
Maybe he would be kind.
Maybe he would respect her
And the word "no" would mean something to him.
She kept quiet for so long
That writing this poem
Feels like betrayal.

Honey Pot

Sarah Bellum Mental

Did you think I wouldn't remember you when
the heat becomes a sidewalk fire that curls its tongue at me?
I'm not here to be pretty
for your needs

to smile when asked to
to paint a face that's

pleasant to see
and to say what you think

I mean
and not what I know

I should say.
I'm not here for your

entertainment
your wishes

thrown into
the wishing well

of this sea made body
hoping I'll grant it

but I will never grant
anything that goes

against my wishes.
I am not your eyelash

to pluck from
stunted eyelids

and wish that I was

→

something else

less loud
less take it or

leave it already.
I am not your trash

sitting outside the door
waiting to be picked up

at a time
more opportune to you.

I am not wasted demands that
your hands keep dipping into

the honey
of this pot.

Trigger Warning

Trigger Warning

These Specified Offences

JLM Morton

10 / 11 / 1985

Male. Supermarket.
Flashing penis folds of honey
roast ham

peekaboo!

between the aisles.

Squeaking soles …--…
  Morse for
make / me / disappear.

16 / 04 / 1987

A gorge on the French exchange,
trailing me down wooded paths,
my breath cracking
branches
off
   the trees.

21 / 06 / 1994

You dirty little slag, or was it slut, I can't
remember now, nothing but the toothy leering
at my neck, the sweat and smoke, the packed-out pub
slutty   glee   globby spits of beer dripping through
my hair. College posh boys, chinos, deck shoes,
venison and Pimm's.

06 / 05 / 2004

top hat wedding by the sea
dressed up: silk jacket tailored

→

  so unlike me   not
recalling I'd said yes   when I
 was dragged across low tide
back against the rocks

I kicked away before he came
inside my mother named me
a disgrace

14 / 2 / 2008

seaman on shore leave
slipped it in my drink

black

out

31 / 01 / 2015

Lunging for me
slut in my own home
the uninvited neighbour
body barging me to bed.

I'm not saying it's right   but
I can still recall the fire
power in my arms
semiautomatic   shoving

through the rooms
launching from the door,
his stone step side smash,

the remembered burning
in my body. My hysterical

strength.

→

28 / 08 / 2020

And lately I'd been thinking I was done.

But still they come
these days by fiber optics.

Dominatrix, PVC
fantasies of drowning me.

Trigger Warning

All Three Of My Rapists Work For Amazon

Sarah Herrin

I was raped
And a friend texts three knife emojis
And my aunt wants to beat the shit out of him
And a friend wouldn't piss on them if they were on fire

I was raped
And a friend says I should report
And my brother offers to call the hotline
And a friend immediately texts her police friend

I was raped
And my husband buys me ice cream
And a friend takes me out for ramen
And my mother wants to get on a plane

I was raped
And a friend feels sick to his stomach
And a friend is heartbroken
And a friend wants to know what he can do

I was raped
And a friend says her sister was too
And more friends say they were too
And a friend's girlfriend asks about me throughout the day

I was raped
And a friend wants to know when there is justice
And my friends say I am brave
And my friends say they love me

I was raped
And it was a friend who raped me.

Your Body Is A Crime Scene / Safe Place

Sarah Herrin

The nurse takes pictures of your entire body
Asks if you've used any mouthwash

Step outside and turn left on the sidewalk
Run one half mile down California Avenue

She swabs the inside of your mouth and lips
Under each of your fingernails

Wait at the cross walk
Run left about a mile down Fauntleroy

She dabs blue dye on your labia
Checks the inside of your uterus

Underneath blooming magnolia trees
Pink and swollen with Spring

You learn that DNA remains on skin for up to 7 days
Even when you've showered and scrubbed twice

Follow the curving road around
To the entrance of Lincoln Park

You find little bruises in new places every day
Forget how to feel safe in your own body

Disappear into the overflowing foliage
Fade into the soothing shadows of old growth forest

You want to wear a tank top but feel too anxious
Although you wore a plain black t-shirt that night

Kneel on the carpeted forest floor
Greet your sacred White Tiger Guardian

107

Trigger Warning

You see your naked body in the mirror and remember
You smell sweat and remember

Bury your face in her body heat
Dry your salty tears in her silky fur

You see a bearded man and remember
You see a dark-haired woman and remember

Cradle the infant version of yourself
Whisper safety until she stops crying

Someone mentions Guinness and you remember
Someone mentions Ardbeg and you remember

Wrap your arms around the teenage version of yourself
She doesn't need to be angry and alone anymore

You can't find a reason to get out of bed again
Your limbs are so heavy – everything hurts

Stand on your own two feet again
Barefoot and bathed in the filtered light through the leaves

Surrounded by love and protection
In your safe place again – your safe place is within.

Trigger Warning

Beasts Of North London

Chloe Laws

They ride to Arsenal games on orange carriages

I'm coming home from an office where no office should be
Oxford Circus

One tells me he'd fuck me
And my mum
She's not with me but I agree

You probably would

Trigger Warning

CONTRIBUTORS

Erin Darcy is a self-taught artist living in Ireland. She is the author of In Her Shoes – Women of the Eighth, an anthology which compiles the stories of women in Ireland under the draconian laws of the 8th Amendment and tells the power of storytelling for changing a nation. Find out more on Instagram @edarcydesign and online www.edarcydesign.com.

Cat Balaq is a poet and body psychotherapist. She is shortlisted for the Bridport Poetry Prize, recipient of the Binstead Prize and Lyra finalist in 2021. Her poetry play Fuck the Moon was shortlisted for the Bristol Old Vic Open Sessions 2019. She writes on themes of trauma and body.

Hackney based author **Catherine Bartram** is of Irish heritage and was raised on a diet of Emily Bronte and Fay Weldon. Catherine's writing centres on the dark themes of the heart and mind; with women's internal voices a central narrative. Impacted by the DV she witnesses as a child; and later herself. Catherine's authentic voice hits hard as she searches for the female power within.

Seneca Basoalto is an Iberian Sicilian poet who has been writing and practicing poetry for three decades. Taking great pride in the evolution of her craft, Seneca has adapted her experiences into candid poetic portraits full of enigmatic devotion and temperamental narratives within her diverse range of work.

Sarah Bellum Mental looks to amplify her voice for those who need a voice to speak on tough subjects. She provides workshops to access creativity for writers. She is an author of two poetry books taking orders now. Connect with her on Instagram @SarahMentalPoet or visit her website for more www.sarahbellummental.com.

Jaimee Boake (she/her) is a high school English Language Arts, Creative Writing, and Leadership Teacher in Sherwood Park, Alberta (Treaty 6 Territory). She loves reading, writing, spending time with her dogs, and is happiest, always, in the mountains. A recipient of the Martin Godfrey Award for Young Writers, more of her work can be found in various literary magazines and anthologies or on Instagram @jaimeeannethology.

Sarah Brooks lives among the ancient redwoods of far Northern California. She is currently pursuing an MA in English/Lit at Mills College in Oakland. Her poetry has been published in Lucky Jefferson, The North Coast Journal, Poetically Magazine's blog, and a collection of pandemic poems called Behind the Mask. Connect with her on Instagram @sarahbneaththemoon.

Victoria Davies is a musician, teacher and writer. Over the past year she has turned her pen (well, smartphone) to writing poetry. She writes about everything and anything, with motherhood a favourite topic. Follow her work on Instagram at @victoriaverses where you will find a warm welcome.

Grace Dellis has been writing poetry for two decades. Her writing has been featured in The Post Grad Journal and ABC Radio National's podcast Soul Search. Grace lives in Australia with her husband and two children; you can connect with her on Instagram @gracedellis.

Tetyana Denford is a Ukrainian-American historical fiction author, poet, and translator. Her first novel, Motherland, was longlisted for the Reader's Digest Self-Published Book Awards and has been published globally to critical acclaim. Her writing has been featured on Elle.com, Vogue, Frontline News, and Medium, and Tetyana also hosts The Craft and Business of Books on YouTube— all about how to navigate the creative process of writing a book and understanding the publishing industry. More recently, Tetyana has published an anthology series of poetry and prose 'Conversation With...' books that explore themes of grief and motherhood. The third in the series, 'Conversation With Love', will be published in 2022. Connect with her on Instagram @tetyanawrites.

Stephanie Farrell-Moore is an actor, voiceover artist, writer and Mother. Her poetry reflects all aspects of womanhood with a particular passion for the power of the menstrual cycle and its impact on identity and creativity. She is currently training with the Red School to become a Menstrual Leadership Mentor.

Eleanor Fatharly is an MA student at The University of Lincoln studying Creative Writing. Her honesty and vulnerability can be seen throughout her experimental poetry as she tries to grow through her uncertain, early twenties. Connect with her on Twitter @ellie_fatharly.

Kristina Rose Garcia has been writing poetry and prose for over 15 years and creating art in various mediums her whole life. She majored in creative writing at Lehman College and was among the first writers to be published in Obscura, the college's literary magazine. She serves the community as a life coach, improving lives and helping others find their voice and inner peace. She hopes to inspire others to follow their passion no matter the obstacles.

Yvonne Gavan is a British journalist - who's written for a wide range of publications including The Telegraph, The Independent, Stylist and Breathe - and a poet who holds an MA in Creative Writing. She is also the host and creator of The Tenderness Revolution, an interview style podcast that asks a range of high profile guests to discuss a moment of tenderness that shaped the course of their lives. Since leaving the UK in 2013, Yvonne has moved around the world from the Caribbean to Botswana in Southern Africa where she is currently based with her husband and three children. Connect with her on instagram @threekindsofsunshine and @thetendernessrevolution.

Sarah Herrin (she/her) is a queer poet based in Boulder, Colorado. She achieved a BFA at the Savannah College of Art & Design, majoring in Sequential Art and Creative Writing, and studied abroad in Southern France – twice. She is a cat-mom, gemologist, and Bowie-lover. Sarah is also the co-founder of Beyond The Veil Press @beyondtheveilpress advocating for mental health awareness through poetry and art.

Whether by profession as a social worker or through her poetry, **Melanie Hess** strives to take people on an interior emotional journey while also allowing them to step outside themselves and see the world differently. We can heal and honour ourselves and join with others through the power of words. Connect with her on Instagram @alohamonkey.

Ivana Kalaš is a pissed-off poet. She constitutes multitudes and lets her words do the talking. Currently, she writes for baghawat.com.

R S Kendle is a poet and writer from the north-east of Scotland. She holds a BA Honours in English Literature and Politics from the University Of Strathclyde. Her work has been published in several issues of Feminist Space Camp, The Survivor Zine, and The Wanderlust Within. Connect with her on Instagram @rskendle.

Chloe Laws is a poet, writer, journalist, and editor from London, best known for her vulnerable poetry and emotive first-person features.

Chloe is the Social Media Director of GLAMOUR Magazine and the Founder and Editor of the online feminist magazine FGRLS CLUB. Connect with her on Instagram @chloegracelaws.

Writer and feminist Social Justice Witch **Kate MacAlister** has been writing poetry for over a decade. Her imaginative works have been published in journals and anthologies all over the world. Her poems are stories of human connection and the dreams of revolution. Find Kate on Instagram @kissed.by_fire.

Tahlia McKinnon is a wild writer, myth-maker and the Founding Editor-In-Chief of Hecate Magazine. Her horror-leaning prose often centres on sex, death and the sacrilegious. This work has been placed in The Daily Drunk Mag, Wrongdoing Magazine, Anti-Heroin Chic and others. You can find her online @tahliamckinnon and via tahliamariamckinnon.co.uk.

JLM Morton's first pamphlet Lake 32 is published by Yew Tree Press (2020). Juliette is recipient of an Arts Council DYCP grant, working towards a collection exploring cloth and colonialism. She is poet in residence for Stroudwater Textile Trust. For more info visit her website www.jlmmorton.com.

Sophia Murray is a mother, witch and poet in the frozen wilderness of Northumberland. She uses words to organise the scrambled eggs that live inside her head. You can see her work on Instagram at @sim_poetry.

Abigail Ottley lives in Penzance. Over the past decade, her work has appeared in more than two hundred outlets, most recently in Impspired, Poetry Wivenhoe, Ink, Sweat & Tears and Paws Poetry. A Pushcart nominee in 2013, Abigail was shortlisted for both the Cinnamon and Three Trees pamphlet awards in 2021.

Kait Quinn is a law admin and poet. Her poetry has appeared in Blood Moon Journal, Polemical Zine, Chestnut Review, VERSES, and various anthologies. She has also self-published four poetry collections. Kait lives in Minneapolis with her partner and their regal cat Spart. Find out more on her website www.kaitquinn.com.

Cc Rose is a first generation, migrant, London poet. Her writings are based on personal experience and her response towards social, economic, racial, environmental and gender issues. Her writing and music hope to invite discussion and invoke connection. From her word, through paper into the hearts of her readers, she welcomes you into the world of her creative thoughts.

Holly Ruskin is a mama and lover of women's words. A freelance writer and Film lecturer, her work includes editing books and screenplays, writing essays and poetry. Her words can be found in various publications; a collection of her poems on motherhood have been featured in the Amazon bestseller Not The Only One. She is co-founder and Editor-in-chief of blood moon POETRY, as well as being a regular contributor and columnist for Motherscope and Sunday Mornings at the River. Connect with her on Instagram @hollyruskin_.

Solo is a poet hell-bent on crafting her own salvation: she uses her verse to exhume personal experiences of trauma and spirituality, examining how the two interplay. Her debut chapbook, Road Trips To Nowhere, was published by Beliveau Books in 2021. She can be found across the internet at @scryingsolo.

Amy Soricelli has been published in numerous publications/ anthologies including Remington Review, The Westchester Review, Literati Magazine, The Muddy River Poetry Review, Glimpse Poetry, *Carmen has No Umbrella but Went for Cigarettes Anyway, Dancing Girl Press 9/2021 *Sail Me Away, Dancing Girl Press, 10/2019. Nominated twice; "Best of the Net."

Rosie Szumowski lives in London with her boyfriend and their cat. She is passionate about women and children's rights, and education around gender based inequalities. You can find her @rosieszumowski on Instagram.

Emma Taylor is a policy adviser and former social worker. She has spent the last decade working for women, children and families who have been through far too much. Emma scribbles poems, stories and occasional articles. Connect with her @taylored_88 for poetry and writing projects.

Originally from Scotland, **Claire Thom** currently lives in the south of Spain where she works as an English teacher and examiner. Claire loves languages and has been writing poetry since she was a child. To read her poetry and find out about her creative projects, follow her on Instagram @poetrycadiz.

Trigger Warning

About blood moon POETRY

blood moon POETRY is a small indie press and a home for poetry written by women from all walks of life. Born from a desire to find and nurture talent that would otherwise go unheard, we specialise in the compilation, editing and publication of collections centred on themes of womanhood. Our bi-annual digital journal also features work from our online community of female poets, authors and illustrators from around the world. In seeking out new and undiscovered creative women, our mission is to amplify their voices to ensure we are the place where women can be heard above the noise.

Connect with us on Instagram @bloodmoonpoetrypress and
Twitter @bloodmoonpoetry
Find us and subscribe at www.bloodmoonpoetry.com

Trigger Warning

About Rape Crisis England & Wales

Rape Crisis England & Wales (RCEW) is a feminist organisation and the national membership body for our network of 39 autonomous member Rape Crisis Centres.

Rape Crisis Centres provide frontline specialist, independent and confidential services for women and girls of all ages who've experienced any form of sexual violence, at any time in their lives. Last year, Centres provided over 650,000 sessions of counselling, advocacy and support.

We exist to support, improve and represent specialist Rape Crisis services, and to amplify the voices and promote the needs and rights of women and girls who have experienced sexual violence and abuse of any kind at any time.

We also raise awareness and understanding of sexual violence and abuse – among the wider community, in the media and with government – and work in partnership with others, for the benefit of all sexual violence and abuse survivors and victims.

Our ultimate vision is a world where everyone is free from the fear and experience of sexual violence and abuse.

Support for survivors:
If you have experienced sexual violence or abuse of any kind, support is available. Whether it happened recently or a long time ago, or if you're not sure what happened, we are here for you.

You can contact the Rape Crisis National Telephone Helpline on 0808 802 9999 (open daily 12pm – 2.30pm and 7pm – 9.30pm). It offers confidential emotional support, information and referral details.
Our Online Live Chat Helpline can be accessed Monday – Friday (various times) via our website rapecrisis.org.uk/get-help/want-to-talk
To find your closest Rape Crisis Centre for counselling, advocacy and further support, visit rapecrisis.org.uk/get-help/want-to-talk
We will listen to you. We will believe you.

Other titles from blood moon POETRY

Faces of Womanhood Edited by Holly Ruskin

A collection of poems about womanhood written by female poets, this anthology is an exploration of what it means to be a woman. Featuring the words of 50 women, Faces of Womanhood is the journey to and from contemporary womanhood. Faces, places and ages are explored in ways unique to each woman and poet. Their work captures and (momentarily) pins down the 21st century mother, sister, wife and daughter, so that this collection can be read as a timeless study and celebration of our differing experiences. A book that draws together voices from all walks of life, Faces of Womanhood is the perfect place to meet yourself, the women you have known and are yet to discover.

This Skin I'm In by Ebony Gilbert

This Skin I'm In is a vulnerable exploration of what it means to be a woman living in a body - her body, and surviving with it through trauma, shame and addiction. A full frontal and an excavation of the soul, each poem is a love letter written by the author to herself and any woman who has ever felt the loneliness and pain of survival. They are also a declaration of tenacity and victory written by a mother, sister, friend and little girl. This is not just a collection of poems but a handbook for survivors.

Silver Hare Tales by Lauren Thomas

Silver Hare Tales is a journey through the author's family history; it's the retelling of ancestral stories and the charting of a return to her womanhood. It speaks to the idea of a woman's longing for where she came from. The lands that birthed our mother's mothers; smells and sounds just tangible as we cross the line between sleep and dream. Grounded in truth, warmth and emotion this book is a treat to heat your bones and a reminder to all women that our strength lies in being rooted.

All available in paperback on Amazon. To purchase visit our website www.bloodmoonpoetry.com/print

Printed in Great Britain
by Amazon